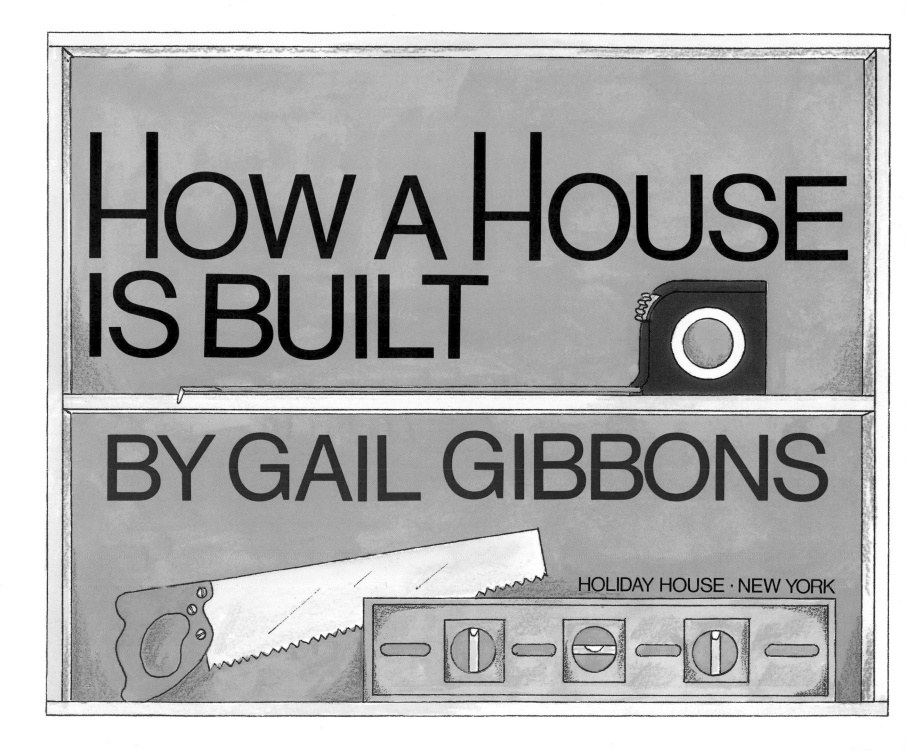

How a House is Built

Is Built

By Gail Gibbons

HOLIDAY HOUSE · NEW YORK

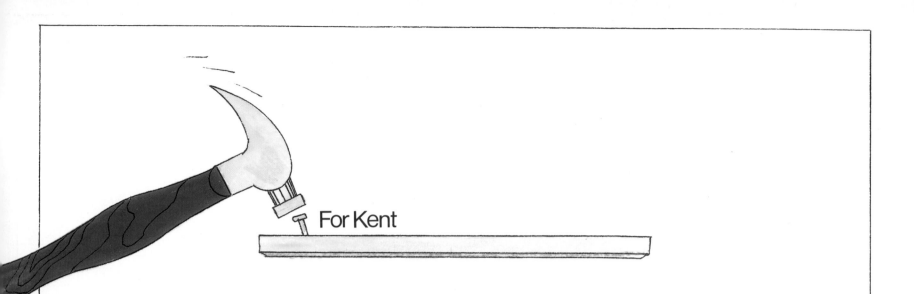

For Kent

Copyright © 1990 by Gail Gibbons
All rights reserved
Printed and Bound in November 2016 at Tien Wah Press, Johor Bahru, Malaysia

18 20 22 24 25 23 21 19

Library of Congress Cataloging-in-Publication Data
Gibbons, Gail.
How a house is built / written and illustrated
by Gail Gibbons. — 1st ed.
p.   cm.
Summary: Describes how the surveyor,
heavy machinery operators, carpenter crew, plumbers,
and other workers build a house.
ISBN 0-8234-0841-8
1. House construction—Juvenile literature.
[1. House construction.]   I. Title.
TH4811.5.G53   1990
690'.837—dc20   90-55107   CIP   AC
ISBN 0-8234-0841-8
ISBN 0-8234-1232-6 (pbk.)

ISBN -13 : 978-0-8234-0841-2 (hardcover)
ISBN -13 : 978-0-8234-1232-7 (paperback)

Many people live in houses.

There are many kinds of houses.

They are built with different materials.

Houses are built in many shapes and sizes, too.

architect

This is how a wood frame house is built. First, an architect draws plans.

The architect recommends a general contractor, who will be in charge of building the house. During the months ahead, the general contractor will hire all these people to complete the project.

The general contractor makes sure everything is done according to schedule.

surveyor

transit

At the construction site, the surveyor measures for the foundation. He hammers wooden stakes into the ground where the corners of the house will be. A well is being drilled.

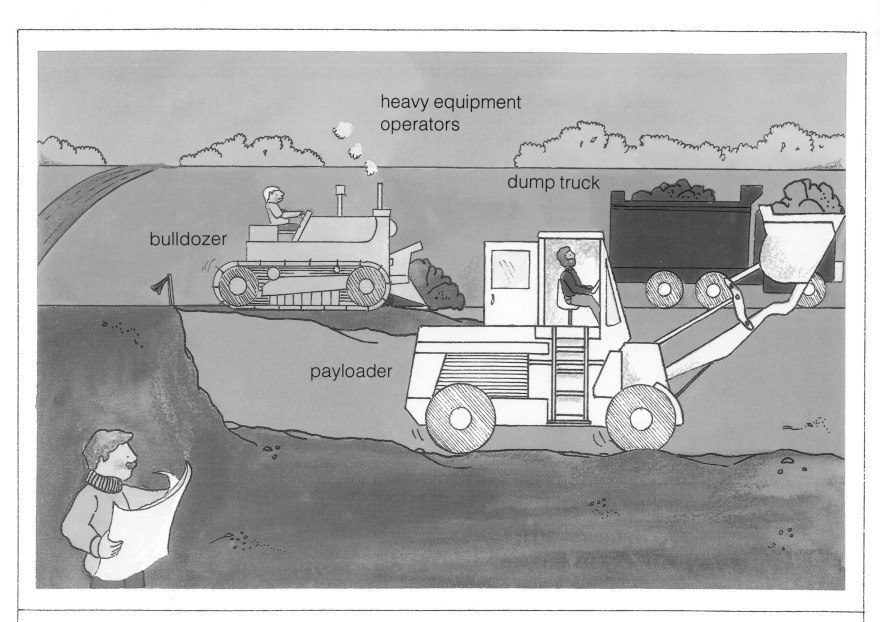

The heavy equipment operators come rumbling up the road.
They dig a hole where the foundation will go. The foundation
will support the weight of the house.

concrete trucks

foundation builders

form

Next, the foundation builders arrive. They dig trenches around the edges. Then they line the trenches with boards to make a form. Trucks move into place and pour concrete.

footing

When the concrete is hard, the boards are removed. This is the footing for the foundation. The footing will give the house a firm base.

gravel

drain

bull float

Then the foundation builders build forms on the footing for the foundation walls. The concrete trucks come and go to fill the forms. The concrete floor of the basement is poured and smoothed over.

The forms are removed when the concrete is hard. Tar is smoothed on the outside walls so moisture can't get inside. Then the bulldozer pushes, or backfills, the dirt up against the outside of the foundation.

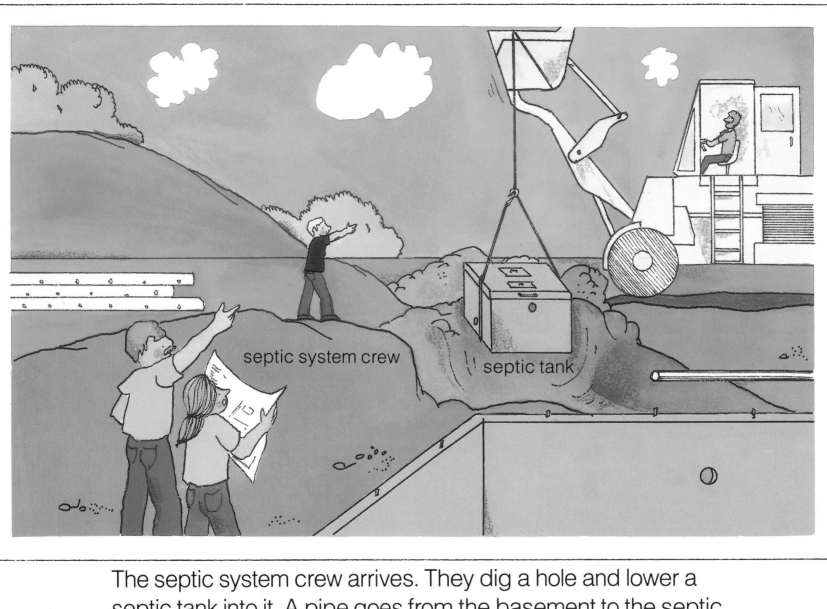

septic system crew

septic tank

The septic system crew arrives. They dig a hole and lower a septic tank into it. A pipe goes from the basement to the septic tank. The waste from drains in the house will flow into the septic tank.

Here comes the carpenter crew. Out come their tools! They bolt down boards, called the sill, to the top of the foundation. Then they hammer heavier boards, called joists, into place.

deck

The carpenters nail sheets of plywood to the joists, making
what is called a deck. It is the floor of the house.

Next, they begin to frame the house. They study the architect's plans. They saw pieces of wood to their correct sizes. They nail together an outside wall of the house. The carpenter crew pushes the wall up and nails it into place.

Another wall goes up...and another!

Finally, all the walls are in place.

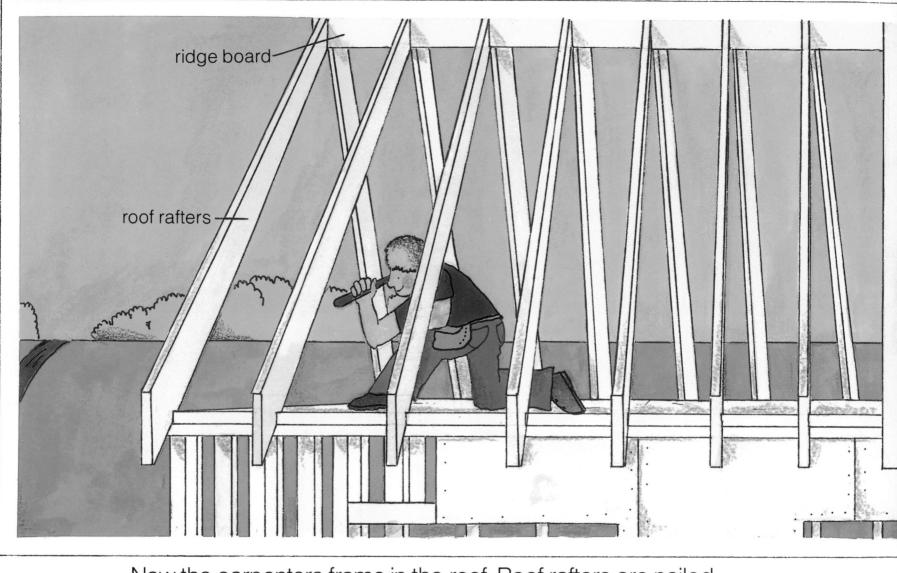

ridge board

roof rafters

Now the carpenters frame in the roof. Roof rafters are nailed to the ridge board. Soon the framing of the house will be complete.

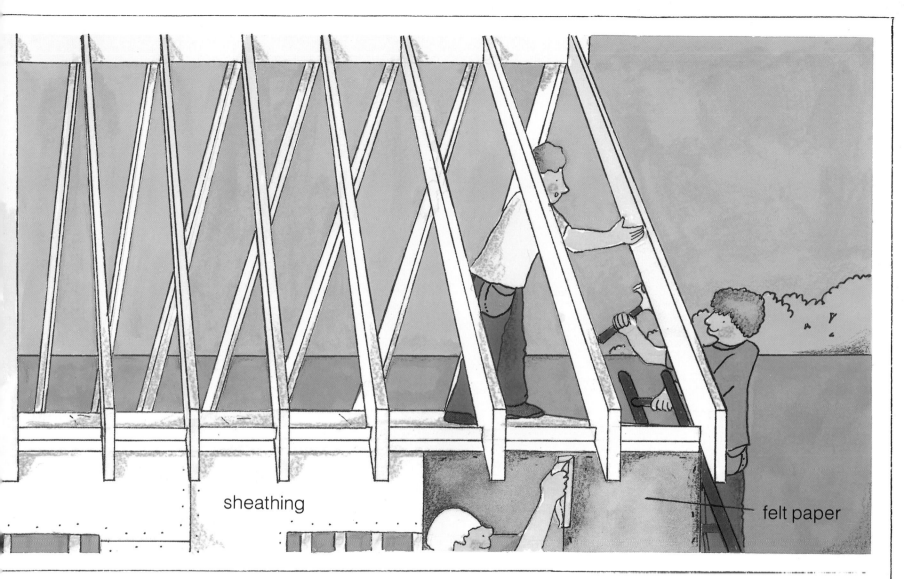

sheathing

felt paper

They begin to enclose the house by nailing sheets of plywood to the outside of the frame. This is called sheathing. Then they saw out the spaces for the windows and doors. Felt paper is nailed to the outside of the plywood to keep moisture out.

shingle

clapboard

On the roof a carpenter is busy nailing down shingles. Other carpenters nail clapboard siding to the sides of the house. Day after day the work continues.

The mason is almost finished building the chimney. Windows
and doors are installed.

Inside the house, interior walls are nailed into place. An electrician runs wire through the walls to outlets and switches. Plumbers install the pipes that bring water to faucets and carry waste from drains to the septic system.

drywall crew

switch

insulation

joint compound

Insulation is tucked between studs to keep heat inside the house. The drywall crew cuts and nails the drywall into place. They smear joint compound onto the drywall joints to make smooth walls.

Next, the finished floors are nailed down. Windows and doors
are trimmed. The painters paint the walls.

heating
specialists

Everything is almost done! The electrician hooks up the
light fixtures. Cabinets are installed. The plumber puts in
the bath tub, toilets and sinks. The furnace and hot air ducts
are installed.

Outside, the landscapers notice that the grass they planted is beginning to grow. They dig a hole for one more bush.

For many months this has been a very busy place. At last the work is done. Now the house is ready to become a home.

SIMPLE SHELTERS OF THE PAST

CAVE

Many years ago some people lived in caves.

IGLOO

An igloo was built using blocks of ice.

EARTH HUT

Some early shelters were built of earth.

TIPI

A tipi was made from animal skins and wooden poles.

Others were made of bark and branches.

BAMBOO SHELTER

A bamboo shelter was built from bamboo poles and a grass roof.

BARK HUT

GRASS HUT

A grass hut was made of grass and branches.

TENT

Cloth and wooden poles were used to build tents.